MY
CONVERSION

My
Conversion

Charles H. Spurgeon

W *Whitaker House*

All Scripture quotations are taken from the *King James Version* (KJV) of the Bible.

MY CONVERSION

ISBN: 0-88368-405-5
Printed in the United States of America
Copyright © 1996 by Whitaker House

Whitaker House
30 Hunt Valley Circle
New Kensington, PA 15068

2 3 4 5 6 7 8 9 10 11 12 / 06 05 04 03 02 01 00 99 98 97

Contents

Chapter 1

Unforgettable Day

I have heard men tell the stories of their conversions and of their spiritual lives in such a way that my heart loathed them and their stories, too. They have told of their sins as if they were boasting in the greatness of their crimes. They have mentioned the love of God, not with a tear of gratitude, not with a heart of thanksgiving, but as if they exalted themselves as much as they exalted God. Oh, when we tell the story of our own conversion, I would have it done differently. We should tell it with great sorrow, remembering what we used to be. We should also tell it with great joy and gratitude, remembering how little we deserve these things.

I was once preaching on conversion and salvation, and I felt, as preachers often do, that it was dry work to tell this story. A dull, dull tale it was to me. Suddenly, the thought crossed my mind, "Why, you are a poor, lost, ruined sinner yourself. Tell it, tell it as you received it. Begin to tell of the grace of God as you trust you feel it yourself." Why, then my eyes began to be fountains of tears. Those hearers who had nodded their heads began to wake up. They listened because they were hearing something that the speaker himself felt and that they recognized as being true to him even if it was not true to them.

Can you not remember, dearly beloved, the day of your salvation? Can you not remember that day of days, that best and brightest of hours, when you first saw the Lord? It was the day you lost your burden, received the roll of promise, rejoiced in full salvation, and went on your way in peace.

My soul can never forget that day. Dying, all but dead, diseased, pained, chained, scourged, bound in fetters of iron, in darkness and the shadow of death, Jesus appeared to me. My eyes looked to Him. The disease was healed, the pains removed, chains were snapped, prison doors were opened, and darkness gave place to light. What delight filled my soul! What mirth, what ecstasy, what sound of music and dancing, what soarings towards heaven, what heights and depths of indescribable delight! Ever since then, I have hardly ever known joys that surpassed the rapture of that first hour.

It is a difficult thing to describe the hour of conversion. It would be easier for my lips to crowd entire poems into one word. It would be easier for my voice to distill hours of melody into a single syllable. It would be easier for my tongue to utter in one letter the essence of the harmony of ages. For the hour of conversion is an hour that surpasses other days of my life as much as gold surpasses dross.

My Conversion

The night of Israel's Passover was a night to be remembered, a theme for poets, and an incessant fountain of grateful song. It is the same way with the time of conversion, the never-to-be-forgotten hour of justification in Jesus and emancipation from guilt. Other days have mingled with their fellow days until, like coins worn in circulation, their image is entirely worn away; but this day remains new, fresh, bright, as distinct in all its parts as if it were but yesterday struck from the mint of time.

Memory will drop from her full hand many a memento that she now cherishes; but she will never, even when she totters to the grave, unbind from her heart the token of the exceedingly happy hour of my redemption. The emancipated galley slave may forget the day that heard his broken shackles rattle on the ground. The pardoned traitor may fail to remember the moment when his life was spared by a pardon. The long-despairing sailor may not recollect the moment when a friendly hand snatched him from the hungry deep. But, hour of forgiven sin, moment of perfect pardon, my soul will never forget you while she has life and being and immortality!

Each day of my life has had its attendant angel, but on this day, like Jacob at Mahanaim, hosts of angels met me. (See Genesis 32:1–2.) The sun has risen every morning, but on that eventful morning it had the light of seven days. As the days of heaven on earth, as the years of immortality, as the ages of glory, as the bliss of heaven, so were the hours of that exceedingly happy day. Rapture divine and ecstasy inexpressible filled my soul. Fear, distress, and grief, with all their train of woes, fled hastily away. In their place joys came without number.

When I was in the hand of the Holy Spirit, under conviction of sin, I had a clear and sharp sense of the justice of God. Sin, whatever it might be to other people, became to me an intolerable burden. It was not so much that I feared hell as that I feared sin. All the while, I had on my mind a deep concern for the honor of God's name and the integrity of

His moral government. I felt that it would not satisfy my conscience if I could be forgiven unjustly. But then there came the question, "How could God be just and yet justify me when I am so guilty?"

I was worried and wearied with this question; neither could I find any answer to it. Certainly, I could never have invented an answer that would have satisfied my conscience. The doctrine of the atonement is to me one of the surest proofs of the divine inspiration of Holy Scripture. Who would or could have thought of the just Ruler dying for the unjust rebel? This is no teaching of human mythology; this is no dream of poetical imagination. This method of atonement is only known among men because it is a fact; fiction could not have devised it. God Himself ordained it; it is not a matter that could have been imagined.

I had heard of the plan of salvation by the sacrifice of Jesus from my youth, but I did not know any more about it in my innermost soul than if I had been born and bred in a remote African tribe. The light was there, but I was blind. It was necessary for the Lord Himself to make the matter plain to me.

It came to me as a new revelation, as fresh as if I had never read in Scripture that Jesus was declared to be the propitiation for sins that God might be just. I believe it will have to come as a revelation to every newborn child of God whenever he sees it—I mean that glorious doctrine of the substitution of the Lord Jesus.

I came to understand that salvation was possible through vicarious sacrifice; furthermore, provision had been made in the first constitution for a substitutionary sacrifice. I was made to see that He who is the Son of God, coequal and coeternal with the Father, had of old been made the covenant Head of a chosen people. In that capacity, He could suffer for them and save them.

Our fall was not at first a personal one, for we fell in our representative, the first Adam. Therefore, it became possible for us to be recovered by a second

Representative, Jesus. He undertook to be the covenant Head of His people so that He could be their second Adam. I saw that before I had actually sinned, I had fallen by my first father's sin. I rejoiced that, therefore, it became possible in point of law for me to rise by a second Head and Representative. The fall by Adam left a loophole of escape; another Adam could undo the ruin done by the first.

When I was anxious about the possibility of a just God pardoning me, I understood and saw by faith that He who is the Son of God became man. In His own blessed person, He bore my "sins in his own body on the tree" (1 Pet. 2:24). I saw that "the chastisement of [my] peace was upon him; and with his stripes [I was] healed" (Isa. 53:5). It was because the Son of God, supremely glorious in His matchless person, undertook to vindicate the law by bearing the sentence due to me, that therefore God was able to pass by my sin.

My sole hope for heaven lies in the full atonement made on Calvary's cross for the ungodly. On that I firmly rely. I do not have the shadow of a hope anywhere else. By myself, I could never have overcome my own sinfulness. I tried and failed. My evil tendencies were too many for me until, in the belief that Christ died for me, I cast my guilty soul on Him. Then I received a conquering principle by which I overcame my sinful self.

The doctrine of the Cross can be used to slay sin, even as the old warriors used their huge two-handed swords and mowed down their foes at every stroke. There is nothing like faith in the sinners' Friend; it overcomes all evil. If Christ has died for me, ungodly as I am, without strength as I am, then I cannot live in sin any longer. I must arouse myself to love and serve Him who has redeemed me. I cannot trifle with the evil that killed my best Friend. I must be holy for His sake. How can I live in sin when He has died to save me from it?

There was a day, as I took my walks abroad, when I came near a spot forever engraved on my memory. There I saw this Friend, my best, my only Friend, murdered. I stooped down in sad alarm and looked at Him. I saw that His hands had been pierced with rough, iron nails, and His feet had been torn in the same way. There was misery in His dead countenance so terrible that I hardly dared to look at it. His body was emaciated with hunger. His back was red with bloody scourges. His brow had a circle of wounds about it; clearly, His brow had been pierced by thorns.

I shuddered, for I had known this Friend very well. He never had a fault; He was the purest of the pure, the holiest of the holy. Who could have injured Him? He never injured any man. All His life He "went about doing good" (Acts 10:38). He had healed the sick; He had fed the hungry; He had raised the dead. For which of these works did they kill Him?

He had never breathed out anything but love. As I looked into the poor, sorrowful face, so full of agony and yet so full of love, I wondered who could have been a wretch so vile as to pierce hands like His. I said to myself, "Where can these traitors live? Who are these who could have killed such a One as this?" Had they murdered an oppressor, we might have forgiven them. Had they slain one who had indulged in vice or villainy, it might have been his just desert. Had it been a murderer or one who had started a revolt, we would have said, "Bury his corpse; justice has at last given him his due."

However, when You were slain, my Best, my only Beloved, where lodged the traitors? Let me seize them, and they will be put to death. If there are torments that I can devise, surely they will endure them all.

Oh, what jealousy, what revenge I felt! If I could only find these murderers, what I would do to them!

As I looked at that corpse, I heard a footstep, and I wondered where it came from. I listened, and I clearly perceived that the murderer was close at hand. It was dark, and I groped about to find him. I found that, somehow or other, wherever I put out my hand, I could not grab him, for he was nearer to me than my hand would go. At last, I put my hand on my own breast. "I have you now," said I. Yes, he was in my own heart. The murderer was hiding within my own bosom, dwelling in the recesses of my inmost soul.

Ah, then I wept indeed that I, in the very presence of my murdered Master, would be harboring the murderer. While I bowed over His corpse, I felt that I was very guilty, and I sang that plaintive hymn:

> 'Twas you, my sins, my cruel sins,
> His chief tormentors were;
> Each of my crimes became a nail,
> And unbelief the spear.

Amid the mob that hounded the Redeemer to His doom, there were some gracious souls whose bitter anguish sought vent in wailing and lamentations—fit music to accompany that march of woe. When my soul can, in imagination, see the Savior bearing His cross to Calvary, it joins the godly women and weeps with them. Indeed, there is true cause for grief—cause lying deeper than those mourning women thought.

They bewailed innocence mistreated, goodness persecuted, love bleeding, meekness about to die; but my heart has a deeper and more bitter cause to mourn. My sins were the scourges that lacerated those blessed shoulders; they crowned those bleeding brows with thorns. My sins cried, "Crucify Him! Crucify Him!" and laid the cross upon His gracious shoulders. His being led forth to die is sorrow enough for one eternity; but my having been His murderer is more, infinitely more, grief than one poor fountain of tears can express.

Why those women loved and wept, it is not hard to guess, but they could not have had greater reasons for love and grief than my heart has. The widow of Nain saw her son restored (see Luke 7:11–15), but I myself have been raised to newness of life. Peter's mother-in-law was cured of the fever (see Matthew 8:14–15), but I of the greater plague of sin. Out of Mary Magdalene seven devils were cast (see Mark 16:9), but a whole legion out of me. Mary and Martha were favored with visits from Him (see John 11:19–45), but He dwells with me. His mother bore His body, but He is formed in me, "the hope of glory" (Col. 1:27). Not being behind the holy women in debt, let me not be behind them in gratitude or sorrow.

> Love and grief my heart dividing,
>   With my tears His feet I'll lave;
> Constant still in heart abiding,
>   Weep for Him who died to save.

William Huntington says in his autobiography that one of the sharpest sensations of pain that he felt, after he had been enlivened by divine grace, was this, "He felt such pity for God." I do not know that I ever heard the expression anywhere else, but it is a very striking one, although I might prefer to say that I have sympathy with God and grief that He should be treated so ill.

Ah, there are many men that are forgotten, that are despised, and that are trampled on by their fellowman. But there never was a man who was so despised as the everlasting God has been! Many a man has been slandered and abused, but never was man abused as God has been. Many have been treated cruelly and ungratefully, but never was one treated as our God has been.

I, too, once despised Him. He knocked at the door of my heart, and I refused to open it. He came to me times without number, morning by morning and night by night. He pricked me in my conscience and spoke to me by His Spirit. When at last the thunders of the law prevailed in my conscience, I thought that Christ was cruel and unkind. Oh, I can never forgive myself that I should have thought so unfavorably of Him!

However, what a loving reception did I have when I went to Him! I thought He would strike me, but His hand was not clenched in anger but opened wide in mercy. I was sure that His eyes would dart lightning-flashes of wrath upon me, but they were full of tears instead. He threw His arms around me and kissed me. He took off my rags and clothed me with His righteousness. He caused my soul to sing aloud for joy. There was also music and dancing in the house of my heart and in the house of His church, because His son that He had lost was found, and he that had been dead was made alive again. (See Luke 15:24.)

There is a power in God's Gospel beyond all description. Once I, like Mazeppa, lashed to the wild horse of my lust, bound hand and foot, incapable of resistance, was galloping on with hell's wolves behind me, howling for my body and my soul as their just and lawful prey. There came a mighty hand that stopped that wild horse, cut my bands, set me down, and brought me into liberty. Is there power in the Gospel? Oh, there is, and he who has felt it must acknowledge it.

There was a time when I lived in the old, strong castle of my sins and rested in my own works. There came a trumpeter to the door and asked me to open it. Angrily, I scolded him from the porch; I said he never would enter. Then there came a pleasant Personage with a loving look. His hands were marked with scars where nails had been driven, and His feet had nail-prints, too. He lifted up His cross, using it as a hammer. At the first blow, the gate of my prejudice shook; at the second, it trembled more; at the third, down it fell, and in He came. He said, "Arise, and stand on your feet, for 'I have loved thee with an everlasting love' (Jer. 31:3)."

The Gospel a thing of power! Ah, that it is! It always wears the dew of its youth; it glitters with morning's freshness; its strength and its glory abide forever. I have felt its power in my own heart. I have the witness of the Spirit within my spirit, and I know the Gospel is a thing of might because it has conquered me and made me submit.

> His free grace alone, from the
>   first to the last,
> Hath won my affections, and
>   bound my soul fast.

Chapter 2

How I Found Christ

In my conversion, the key was making the discovery that I had nothing to do but to look to Christ and I would be saved.

I believe that I had been a very good, attentive hearer; my own impression about myself was that nobody ever listened much better than I did. For years, as a child, I tried to learn the way of salvation. Either I did not hear it explained, which I think cannot quite have been the case, or else I was spiritually blind and deaf and hence could not see it or hear it. Either way, the good news that I was, as a sinner, to look away from myself to Christ as much startled me and came as fresh to me as any news I ever heard in my life. Had I ever read my Bible? Yes, I had read it earnestly. Had I ever been taught by Christian people? Yes, I had, by mother and father and others. Had I not heard the Gospel? Yes, I think I had. However, somehow it was like a new revelation to me that I was to believe and live.

I confess that I had been tutored in piety, put into my cradle by prayerful hands, and lulled to sleep by songs about Jesus. I had heard the Gospel continually, with "precept upon precept; line upon line" (Isa. 28:10), here much and there much. Yet, when the Word of the Lord came to me with power, it was as new as if I had lived among the unvisited tribes of Central Africa and had never heard the tidings of the cleansing fountain filled with blood, drawn from the Savior's veins.

When for the first time I received the Gospel and my soul was saved, I thought that I had never really heard it before. I began to think that the preachers to whom I had listened had not truly preached it. But, on looking back, I am inclined to believe that I had heard the Gospel fully preached many hundreds of times before. This was the difference: I then heard it as though I did not hear it. When I did hear it, the message may not have been any more clear in itself than it had been at former times, but the power of the Holy Spirit was present to open my ears and to guide the message to my heart.

I have no doubt that I heard a hundred times such texts as these: "He that believeth and is baptized shall be saved" (Mark 16:16); "Look unto me, and be ye saved, all the ends of the earth" (Isa. 45:22); "As Moses lifted up the serpent in the wilderness, even so must the Son of man be lifted up: that whosoever believeth in Him should not perish, but have eternal life" (John 3:14–15). However, I had no intelligent idea of what faith meant.

When I first discovered what faith really was, I exercised it. I believed as soon as I knew what believing meant.

Then I thought I had never heard the truth preached before. Now I am persuaded that the light shone often on my eyes, but I was blind; therefore, I thought that the light had never come there. The light was shining all the while, but there was no power to receive it. The eyeball of the soul was not sensitive to the divine beams.

I could not believe that it was possible that *my* sins could be forgiven. I do not know why, but I seemed to be the one exception in the world. When the list was made out, it appeared to me that for some reason I must have been left out. If God had saved me and not the world, I would have been surprised indeed; but if He had saved all the world except me, that would have seemed only right to me. And now, being saved by grace, I cannot help saying, "I am indeed 'a brand plucked out of the fire' (Zech. 3:2)!"

I believe that some of us who were kept by God a long time before we found Him, love Him better perhaps than if we had received Him right away. We can preach better to others, and we can speak more of His loving-kindness and tender mercy. John Bunyan could not have written as he did if he had not been dragged around by the Devil for many years. I love that picture of dear old Christian. I know that when I first read *The Pilgrim's Progress* and saw the picture of Christian carrying the burden on his back, I felt so sorry for the poor man that I thought I would jump with joy when, after he had carried his heavy load so long, he at last got rid of it. That was how I felt when the burden of guilt, which I had borne so long, was forever rolled away from my shoulders and my heart.

I can recollect when, like the poor dove sent out by Noah from his hand, I flew over the wide expanse of waters and hoped to find some place where I could rest my wearied wing. (See Genesis 8:6–11.) Up towards the north I flew. My eye looked keenly through the mist and darkness to perhaps find some floating substance on which my soul might rest its foot, but it found nothing. Again it turned its wing and flapped it, but not so rapidly as before, across that deep water that knew no shore. Still there was no rest. The raven had found its resting place on a floating body and was feeding itself on the carrion of some drowned man's carcass, but my poor soul found no rest.

I flew on. I fancied I saw a ship sailing out at sea. It was the ship of the law. I thought I would put my feet on its sail or rest myself on its ropes for a time and thereby find some refuge. But, ah, it was an airy phantom on which I could not rest. My foot had no right to rest on the law. I had not kept it, and the soul that does not keep it must die (Ezek. 18:20).

At last I saw the ship *Christ Jesus*—that happy ark. I thought I would fly there, but my poor wing was weary. I could fly no further. Down I sank. But, as providence would have it, when my wings were feeble and I was falling into the flood to be drowned, just below me was the roof of the ark. I saw a hand stretched out, and One took hold of me and said, "'I have loved thee with an everlasting love' (Jer. 31:3). Therefore, I have not delivered 'the soul of [My] turtledove unto the multitude of the wicked' (Ps. 74:19). Come in, come in!" Then I realized that I had an olive leaf in my mouth. It was an olive leaf of peace with God and peace with man, plucked off by Jesus' mighty power.

Once, God preached to me by an object lesson in the depth of winter. The earth had been black, and there was scarcely a green thing or a flower to be seen. As I looked across the fields, there was nothing but barrenness—bare hedges, leafless trees, and black, black earth—wherever I gazed. Suddenly, God spoke, and He unlocked the treasures of the snow. White flakes descended until there was no blackness to be seen, and all was one sheet of dazzling whiteness. It was the same time that I was seeking the Savior and not long before I found Him. I well remember that sermon that I saw before me in the snow:

Come now, and let us reason together, saith the LORD: though your

*sins be as scarlet, they shall be as
white as snow; though they be red
like crimson, they shall be as wool.*
(Isa. 1:18)

Personally, I have to thank God for
many good books. I thank Him for Dr.
Doddridge's *Rise and Progress of Religion in the Soul,* for Baxter's *Call to the
Unconverted,* for Alleine's *Alarm to Sinners,* and for James's *Anxious Enquirer*.
However, I am most thankful to God,
not for books, but for the preached
Word. I thank Him for the Word addressed to me by a poor, uneducated
man. He was a man who had never received any training for the ministry and
probably will never be heard of in this
life. He was a man engaged in business,
no doubt of a humble kind, during the
week but who had just enough grace to
say on that Sunday, "Look unto me, and
be ye saved, all the ends of the earth"
(Isa. 45:22).

The books were good, but the man
was better. The revealed Word awakened me, but it was the preached Word

that saved me. I must ever attach special value to the hearing of the truth, for by it I received the joy and peace in which my soul delights.

While under concern for my soul, I resolved that I would attend all the places of worship in the town where I lived in order that I might find out the way of salvation. I was willing to do anything and be anything if God would only forgive my sin. I set off, determined to go around to all the churches.

I did go to every place of worship, but for a long time I went in vain. I do not, however, blame the ministers. One man preached divine sovereignty. I could hear him with pleasure, but what was that sublime truth to a poor sinner who wished to know what he must do to be saved? There was another admirable man who always preached about the law, but what was the use of plowing up ground that needed to be sown? Another was a practical preacher. I heard him, but it was very much like a commanding officer teaching the maneuvers of war to a set of men without feet. What could I do? All his exhortations were lost on me. I knew it was said, "Believe on the Lord Jesus Christ, and thou shalt be saved" (Acts 16:31), but I did not know what it meant to believe on Christ.

These good men all preached truths suited to many in their congregations who were spiritually-minded people; however, what I wanted to know was, "How can I get my sins forgiven?" and they never told me that. I desired to hear how a poor sinner, under a sense of sin, can find peace with God; and when I went to church, I heard a sermon on, "Be not deceived; God is not mocked" (Gal. 6:7). Such topics cut me up still worse; they did not bring me into rest. I went again another day, and the text was something about the glories of the righteous; nothing for poor me! I was like a dog under the table, not allowed to eat of the children's food.

I went time after time, and I can honestly say that I do not know that I ever went without prayer to God. Furthermore, I am sure there was not a more attentive hearer than myself in all the place, for I panted and longed to understand how I could be saved.

I sometimes think I might have been in darkness and despair until now if it had not been for the goodness of God in sending a snowstorm one Sunday morning while I was going to a certain church. When I could go no further, I turned down a side street and came to a little Primitive Methodist chapel. In that chapel, there may have been a dozen or fifteen people. I had heard of the Primitive Methodists, how they sang so loudly that they gave people headaches, but that did not matter to me. I wanted to know how I could be saved, and if they could tell me that, I did not care how much they made my head ache.

The minister did not come that morning; he was snowed in, I suppose. At last, a very thin-looking man, a shoemaker or tailor or something of that sort, went up to the pulpit to preach. Now, it is good for preachers to be instructed, but this man was really unintelligent. He was forced to stick to his text for the simple reason that he had little else to say. The text was,

Look unto me, and be ye saved, all the ends of the earth.   (Isa. 45:22)

He did not even pronounce the words correctly, but that did not matter. I thought, "Now there's a glimpse of hope for me in that text."

The preacher began thus: "My dear friends, this is a very simple text indeed. It says, 'Look.' Now, lookin' don't take a deal of pains. It ain't liftin' your foot or your finger; it is just, 'Look.' Well, a man needn't go to college to learn to look. You may be the biggest fool, and yet you can look. A man needn't be wealthy to be able to look. Anyone can look; even a child can look.

"Then the text says, 'Look unto *Me.*' Ay, many of ye are lookin' to yourselves, but it's no use lookin' there. You'll never find any comfort in yourselves. Some look to God the Father. No, look to Him by and by. Jesus Christ says, 'Look unto Me.' Some of ye say, 'We must wait for the Spirit's workin'.' You have no business with that just now. Look to Christ. The text says, 'Look unto Me.'"

Then the good man followed up his text in this way: "Look unto Me; I am sweatin' great drops of blood. Look unto Me; I am hangin' on the cross. Look unto Me; I am dead and buried. Look unto Me; I rise again. Look unto Me; I ascend to heaven. Look unto Me; I am sittin' at the Father's right hand. O poor sinner, look unto Me! Look unto Me!"

When he had managed to go on for ten minutes or so, he was at the end of his resources. Then he looked at me under the gallery. I dare say, with so few present, he knew I was a stranger. Just fixing his eyes on me, as if he knew all my heart, he said, "Young man, you look very miserable." Well, I did, but I was not used to having remarks made from the pulpit on my personal appearance. However, it was a good blow, struck right home.

He continued, "And you always will be miserable—miserable in life and miserable in death—if you don't obey my text. But if you obey now, this moment, you will be saved." Then, lifting up his hands, he shouted, as only a Primitive Methodist could do, "Young man, look to Jesus Christ. Look! Look! Look! You have nothin' to do but to look and live."

I saw at once the way of salvation. I do not know what else he said—I did not take much notice of it—I was so possessed with that one thought. It was similar to when the brazen serpent was lifted up, and the people only looked and were healed (see Numbers 21:6–9); so it was with me. I had been waiting to do fifty things, but when I heard that word, "look," what a charming word it seemed to me! Oh, I looked until I could have almost looked my eyes away!

There and then the cloud was gone; the darkness had rolled away. That moment I saw the sun. That instant I could have sung with the most enthusiastic of them about the precious blood of Christ and the simple faith that looks alone to Him.

Oh, that somebody had told me this before: "Trust Christ and you will be saved." Yet my circumstances were, no doubt, all wisely ordered, and now I can say,

E'er since by faith I saw the stream
Thy flowing wounds supply,
Redeeming love has been my theme,
And shall be till I die.

I do confess from my soul that I was never satisfied until I came to Christ. When I was still a child, I had far more wretchedness than I ever have now. I will even add, more weariness, more care, more heartache than I know at this day. I may be alone in this confession, but I make it and know it to be the truth. Since that dear hour when my soul cast itself on Jesus, I have found solid joy and peace. Before that, all those supposed joys of early youth, all the imagined ease and happiness of boyhood, were only vanity and vexation of spirit to me.

That happy day when I found the Savior and learned to cling to His dear feet was a day I will never forget. An obscure child, unknown, unheard of, I listened to the Word of God, and that precious text led me to the cross of Christ. I can testify that the joy of that day was utterly indescribable. I could have leaped; I could have danced. There was no expression, however fanatical, that would have been out of keeping with the joy of my spirit at that hour.

Many days of Christian experience have passed since then, but there has never been one that has had the full exhilaration, the sparkling delight which that first day had. I thought I could have sprung from the seat on which I sat. I could have called out with the wildest of those Methodist brothers who were present, "I am forgiven! I am forgiven! A monument of grace! A sinner saved by blood!"

My spirit saw its chains broken to pieces. I felt that I was an emancipated soul, an heir of heaven, a forgiven one, accepted in Christ Jesus. "He brought me up also out of an horrible pit, out of the miry clay, and set my feet upon a rock, and established my goings" (Ps.

40:2). I thought I could dance all the way home. I could understand what John Bunyan meant when he declared he wanted to tell the crows on the plowed land all about his conversion. He was too full to hold it in; he felt he must tell somebody.

Not everyone can remember the very day and hour of his deliverance. However, it was the same way with me as it was with Richard Knill. He said, "At such and such a time of the day, clang went every harp in heaven, for Richard Knill was born again." The clock of mercy struck in heaven the hour and moment of my emancipation, for the time had come. Between half-past ten o'clock, when I entered that chapel, and half-past twelve o'clock, when I was back again at home, what a change had taken place in me! I had passed from darkness into marvelous light, from death to life.

Simply by looking to Jesus, I had been delivered from despair. I was brought into such a joyous state of mind that when they saw me at home, they said to me, "Something wonderful has happened to you." I was eager to tell them all about it. Oh, there was joy in the household that day when all heard that the eldest son had found the Savior and knew himself to be forgiven—bliss compared with which all earth's joys are less than nothing and vanity.

Yes, I had looked to Jesus as I was, and I had found in Him my Savior. The eternal purpose of Jehovah had decreed it thus. As, the moment before, there was none more wretched than I was, so, within that second, there was none more joyous. It did not take any longer than a flash of lightning. It was done, and never has it been undone. I looked and lived and leaped in joyful liberty as I beheld my sin punished upon the great Substitute and put away for ever. I looked unto Him as He bled upon that tree. His eyes darted a glance of love unutterable into my spirit, and in a moment I was saved.

Looking unto Him, the bruises that my soul had suffered were healed; the gaping wounds were cured; the broken bones rejoiced; the rags that had covered me were all removed; my spirit was white as the spotless snows of the far-off North. I had melody in my spirit, for I was saved, washed, cleansed, forgiven through Him who hung on the tree.

My Master, I cannot understand how You could stoop Your wondrous head to such a death as the death of the cross. I cannot understand how You could take from Your brow the crown of stars that from eternity past had shone resplendent there, but it astonishes me far more how You could permit the thorn-crown to encircle Your temples. That You would cast away the mantle of Your glory, the azure of Your everlasting empire, I cannot comprehend. But it is even harder to comprehend how You could have become veiled in the ignominious purple for a while to be mocked by impious men, who bowed to You as a pretended king. It is incomprehensible how You could be stripped naked to Your shame, without a single covering, and die a felon's death. But the marvel is that You suffered all this for me! Truly, Your love to me is wonderful, "passing the love of women" (2 Sam. 1:26)!

Was there ever grief like Yours? Was there ever love like Yours, that could open the floodgates of such grief? Was there ever love so mighty as to become the fount from which such an ocean of grief could come rolling down?

There was never anything so true to me as those bleeding hands and that thorn-crowned head. Home, friends, health, wealth, comforts—all lost their luster that day when He appeared, just as stars are hidden by the light of the sun. He was the only Lord and Giver of life's best bliss, the one well of living water "springing up into everlasting life" (John 4:14).

As I saw Jesus on His cross before me, and as I mused upon His sufferings and death, I thought I saw Him cast a look of love on me. Then I looked at Him and cried,

> Jesus, lover of my soul,
> Let me to Thy bosom fly.

He said, "Come," and I flew to Him and clasped Him. When He let me go again, I wondered where my burden was. It was gone! There in the sepulcher it lay, and I felt light as air. Like a winged sylph, I could fly over mountains of trouble and despair. Oh, what liberty and joy I had! I could leap with ecstasy, for I had been forgiven much, and I was freed from sin.

With the spouse in the Song of Solomon, I could say, "I found him" (Song 3:4). I, a lad, found the Lord of glory. I, a slave to sin, found the Great Deliverer. I, the child of darkness, found the Light of Life. I, the uttermost of the lost, found my Savior and my God. I, widowed and desolate, found my Friend, my Beloved, my Husband.

Oh, how amazed I was that *I* was pardoned! It was not the pardon that I was so amazed at; the wonder was that it should come to *me*. I marveled that He was able to pardon such sins as mine, such crimes, so numerous and so dark. I marveled that, after such an accusing conscience, He had power to still every wave within my spirit and make my soul like the surface of a river—undisturbed, quiet, and at ease.

It did not matter to me whether the day itself was gloomy or bright, for I had found Christ; that was enough for me. He was my Savior. He was my all. I can heartily say that one day of pardoned sin was a sufficient recompense for the whole five years of conviction. I have to thank God for every terror that ever scared me by night and for every foreboding that alarmed me by day. It has made me happier ever since; for now, if there is a trouble weighing on my soul, I thank God it is not like the burden of sin and conviction. That was a burden so heavy with distress and affliction that it bowed me to the very earth and made me crawl like a beast. I know I can never again suffer what I have suffered. I can never, unless I were sent to hell, know more agony than I have known. Now, that ease, that joy and peace in believing, that freedom from condemnation that belongs to me as a child of God, is made doubly sweet and inexpressibly precious by remembering my past days of sorrow and grief.

Blessed be God forever, who by those dark days, like a dreary winter, has made these summer days all the fairer and sweeter! I need not walk through the earth fearful of every shadow and afraid of every man I meet, for sin is washed away. My spirit is no longer guilty; it is pure and holy. The frown of God no longer rests on me, but my Father smiles. I see His eyes; they are glancing love. I hear His voice; it is full of sweetness. I am forgiven, I am forgiven, I am forgiven!

When I look back on it, I can see one reason why the Word was blessed to me as I heard it preached in that Primitive Methodist chapel at Colchester. I had been up early crying to God for the blessing. As a boy, when I was seeking the Savior, I used to rise with the sun that I might have time to read gracious books and seek the Lord. I can recall the kind of pleas I used when I took my arguments and came before the throne of grace: "Lord, save me; it will glorify

Your grace to save such a sinner as I am! Lord, save me, or else I am lost to all eternity. Do not let me perish, Lord! Save me, O Lord, for Jesus died! By His agony and bloody sweat, by His cross and passion, save me!" I often proved that the early morning was the best part of the day. I liked those prayers of which the psalmist said, "In the morning shall my prayer prevent thee" (Ps. 88:13).

Chapter 3

Assurance of Salvation

The Holy Spirit, who enabled me to believe, gave me peace through believing. I felt as sure that I was forgiven as before I felt sure of condemnation. I had been certain of my condemnation because the Word of God declared it and because my conscience bore witness to it. However, when the Lord justified me, I was made equally certain by the same witnesses. The Word of the Lord says, "He that believeth on him is not condemned" (John 3:18). My conscience bore witness that I believed and that God in pardoning me was just.

Thus I had the witness of the Holy Spirit and also of my own conscience, and these two agreed in one.

That great and excellent man, Dr. Johnson, used to hold the opinion that no man ever could know that he was pardoned, that there was no such thing as assurance of faith. Perhaps, if Dr. Johnson had studied his Bible a little more and had had a little more of the enlightenment of the Spirit, he, too, might have come to know his own pardon. Certainly, he was not a very reliable judge of theology any more than he was of porcelain, which he once attempted to make but never succeeded. I think both in theology and porcelain his opinion is of very little value.

How can a man know that he is pardoned? There is a text that says, "Believe on the Lord Jesus Christ, and thou shalt be saved" (Acts 16:31). I believe on the Lord Jesus Christ; is it irrational to believe that I am saved? Christ said, "He that believeth on the Son hath everlasting life" (John 3:36). I believe on Christ; am I absurd in believing that I have eternal life? I find the apostle Paul speaking by the Holy Ghost and saying, "There is therefore now no condemnation to them which are in Christ Jesus" (Rom. 8:1). "Being justified by faith, we have peace with God" (Rom. 5:1). If I know that my trust is fixed on Jesus only and that I have faith in Him, were it not ten thousand times more absurd for me not to be at peace than for me to be filled with joy unspeakable? When we take God at His Word, we know that we are saved. Knowing is a necessary consequence of faith.

I took Jesus as my Savior, and I was saved. I can tell the reason that I took Him for my Savior. To my own humiliation, I must confess that I did it because I could not help it; it was the only thing I could do. That stern law-work had hammered me into such a condition that, if there had been fifty other saviors, I could not have thought of them—I was driven to this One. I wanted a Divine Savior. I wanted One who was made a curse for me to atone for my guilt. I wanted One who had died, for I deserved to die. I wanted One who had risen again, who was able by His life to make me live. I wanted the exact Savior that stood before me in the Word, revealed to my heart, and I could not help having Him.

I could then understand the language of Rutherford when, being full of love to Christ, once upon a time in the dungeon of Aberdeen he said, "O my Lord, if there were a broad hell between me and You, if I could not get to You except by wading through it, I would not think twice, but I would go through it all, if I could only embrace You and call You mine!"

Oh, how I loved Him! Passing all loves except His own was that love that I felt for Him then. If, beside the door of the place in which I met with Him, there had been a stake of blazing logs, I would have stood upon them without chains, glad to give my flesh and blood and bones to be ashes that would testify my love to Him. Had He asked me then to give all my possessions to the poor, I would have given all and thought myself to be amazingly rich in having beggared myself for His name's sake. Had He commanded me then to preach in the midst of all His foes, I could have said,

> There's not a lamb in all Thy flock
> I would disdain to feed;
> There's not a foe, before whose face
> I'd fear Thy cause to plead.

Has Jesus saved *me?* I dare not speak with any hesitation here; I *know* He has. His Word is true; therefore, I am saved. My evidence that I am saved does not lie in the fact that I preach or that I do this or that. All my hope lies in this: "Christ Jesus came...to save sinners" (1 Tim. 1:15). I am a sinner, and I trust Him; thus, He came to save me, and I am saved. I live habitually in the enjoyment of this blessed fact. It has been a long time since I have doubted the truth of it, for I have His own Word to sustain my faith.

Salvation is a very surprising thing—a thing to be marveled at most of all by those who enjoy it. I know that it is to me even to this day the greatest wonder that I ever heard of, that God would ever justify *me*. I feel that I am a lump of unworthiness, a mass of corruption, and a heap of sin, apart from His almighty love. Nevertheless, I know, by a full assurance, that I am justified by faith that is in Christ Jesus. I am treated as if I had been perfectly just. I am made an heir of God and a joint-heir with Christ. All this I am given, though by nature I must take my place among the most sinful. I, who am altogether undeserving, am treated as if I had been deserving. I am loved with as much love as if I had always been godly, whereas in times past I was ungodly.

I have always considered, with Luther and Calvin, that the sum and substance of the Gospel lies in that word *substitution*—Christ standing in the place of man. If I understand the Gospel, it is this: I deserve to be lost forever; the only reason why I am not damned is that Christ was punished in my place, and there is no need to execute a sentence twice for sin. On the other hand, I know I cannot enter heaven unless I have a perfect righteousness. I am absolutely certain I will never have one of my own, for I find I sin every day. Christ, however, had a perfect righteousness. He said, "There, poor sinner, take My garment and put it on. You will stand before God as if you were Christ, and I will stand before God as if I had been the sinner. I will suffer in the sinner's stead, and you will be rewarded for works that you did not do but that I did for you."

I find it very convenient every day to come to Christ as a sinner as I came the first time. "You are no saint," says the Devil. Well, if I am not, I am a sinner, and "Christ Jesus came into the world to save sinners" (1 Tim. 1:15). Sink or swim, I go to Him; I have no other hope. By looking to Him, I received all the faith that inspired me with confidence in His grace. Moreover, the word that first drew my soul—"look unto me" (Isa. 45:22)—still rings its clarion note in my ears. There I once found conversion, and there I will ever find refreshing and renewal.

Let me tell my personal testimony of what I have seen and what my own ears have heard and what my own heart has tasted. First, Christ is the Only Begotten of the Father. He is divine to me, if He is human to all the world besides; He has done for me what none but a God could do. He has subdued my stubborn will, melted a heart of stone, broken a chain of steel, opened the gates of brass, and snapped the bars of iron. He has turned for me my mourning into laughter and my desolation into joy. He has led my captivity captive and made my heart rejoice with joy unspeakable and full of glory. Let others think what they will of Him; to me He must ever be the Only Begotten of the Father. Blessed be His holy name!

> Oh, that I could now adore Him,
>   Like the heavenly host above,
> Who for ever bow before Him,
>   And unceasing sing His love!
>   Happy songsters!
> When shall I your chorus join?

Again, I testify that He is full of grace. Ah, had He not been, I would never have beheld His glory. I was full of sin to overflowing. I was condemned already because I did not believe on Him. (See John 3:18.) He drew me when I did not want to come, and though I struggled hard, He still continued to draw. When at last I came to His mercy seat, all trembling like a condemned culprit, He said, "Your sins, which are many, are all forgiven you; be of good cheer." (See Luke 7:47.) Let others despise Him, but I bear witness that He is full of grace.

Finally, I bear witness that He is full of truth. True have His promises been; not one has failed. I have often doubted Him; for that I blush. He has never failed me; in this I must rejoice. His promises have been "yea" and "amen" (2 Cor. 1:20). Of course, I am speaking the testimony of every believer in Christ, though I put it personally to make it even more forcible.

I bear witness that no servant ever had such a master as I have; no brother has ever had such a kinsman as He has been to me; no spouse has ever had such a husband as Christ has been to my soul; no sinner a better savior; no soldier a better captain; no mourner a better comforter than Christ has been to my spirit. I want none besides Him. In life, He is my life; and in death, He will be the death of death. In poverty, Christ is my riches. In sickness, He makes my bed. In darkness, He is my Star; and in brightness, He is my Sun.

By faith, I understand that the blessed Son of God redeemed my soul with His own heart's blood. By sweet experience, I know that He raised me up from the pit of dark despair and set my feet on the rock (Ps. 40:2). He died for me. This is the root of every satisfaction I have. He put all my transgressions away. He cleansed me with His precious blood. He covered me with His perfect righteousness. He wrapped me up in His own virtues. While I abide in this world, He has promised to keep me from its temptations and snares. When I depart from this world, He has already prepared for me a mansion in the heaven of unfading bliss and a crown of everlasting joy that will never, never fade away.

To me, then, the days or years of my mortal sojourn on this earth are of little importance. Nor is the way I die of much consequence. If my foes were to sentence me to martyrdom or if physicians were to declare that I must soon depart this life, it is all alike.

> A few more rolling suns at most
> Shall land me on fair Canaan's
>   coast.

While my brief time on earth lasts, what more could I wish for than to be the servant of Him who became the Servant of Servants for me? I can say much good about Christ's religion. If I had to die like a dog with no hope whatsoever of immortality, if I wanted to lead a happy life, let me serve my God with all my heart. Let me be a follower of Jesus and walk in His footsteps. If there were no hereafter, I would still prefer to be a Christian, even the humblest Christian minister, to being a king or an emperor. You see, I am persuaded there are more delights in Christ than are to be found in all the praises of this harlot-world. Yes, there is more joy in one glimpse of His face than in all the delights that the world can yield to us in its sunniest and brightest days. And I am persuaded that what He has been until now, He will be to the end. Where He has begun a good work, He will carry it on. (See Philippians 1:6.)

In the religion of Jesus Christ, there are clusters even on earth too heavy for one man to carry. There are fruits that are so rich that even angel lips have never been sweetened with more luscious wine. There are joys to be had here that are so fair that even the exquisite foods and delicious wine of paradise can scarcely excel the sweets of satisfaction found in the earthly banquets of the Lord.

I have seen hundreds and thousands who have given their hearts to Jesus, but I never did see one who said he was disappointed with Him. I never met one who said Jesus Christ was less than He was declared to be.

When my eyes first beheld Him, when the burden slipped off my heavy-laden shoulders and I was free from condemnation, I thought that all the preachers I had ever heard had not half preached; they had not told half the beauty of my Lord and Master. So good! So generous! So gracious! So willing to forgive! It seemed to me as if they had almost slandered Him. They painted His likeness, doubtless, as well as they could, but it was a mere smudge compared with the matchless beauties of His face. All who have ever seen Him will say the same.

I go back to my home, many a time, mourning that I cannot preach my Master even as I myself know Him, and what I know of Him is very little compared with the matchlessness of His grace. Oh, that I knew more of Him and could tell it better!

Chapter 4

My Experiences after Conversion

Our faith at times has to fight for its very existence. The old Adam within us rages mightily; and the new spirit within us, like a young lion, disdains to be vanquished. These two strong ones contend until our spirit is full of agony.

Some of us know what it is to be tempted with blasphemies we would not dare repeat. We know what it is to be vexed with horrid temptations that we have grappled with and overcome but which have almost cost us resistance unto blood. In such inward conflicts, saints must be alone. They cannot tell their feelings to others; they would not dare. Even if they did, their own fellow Christians would despise or scold them, for most professing Christians would not even know what they meant. Even those who have walked other fiery ways would not be able to sympathize in all cases. They would answer the poor, troubled soul, "These are points in which we cannot go with you."

Christ alone "was in all points tempted like as we are, yet without sin" (Heb. 4:15). Not one man is tempted in all points exactly like another man. Each one has certain trials in which he must stand alone amid the rage of war. He may not even have a book to help him or a biography to assist him, since no man ever went that way before except that one Man, whose trail reveals a nail-pierced foot. He alone knows all the devious paths of sorrow. Yet, even in such byways, the Lord is with us, helping us, sustaining us, and giving us grace to conquer in the end.

When my eyes first looked to Christ, He was a very real Christ to me. When my burden of sin rolled off my back, it was a real pardon and a real release from sin to me. When that day I said for the first time, "Jesus Christ is mine," it was a real possession of Christ to me.

When I went up to the sanctuary in that early dawn of youthful piety, every song was really a psalm. When there was a prayer, oh, how I followed every word! It was a prayer indeed! It was the same way, too, in silent quietude, when I drew near to God. It was no mockery, no routine, no matter of mere duty; it was a real talking with my Father who is in heaven. And oh, how I loved my Savior Christ then! I would have given all I had for Him! How I felt towards sinners that day! Youth that I was, I wanted to preach, and

Tell to sinners round,
What a dear Savior I had found.

One of the greatest sorrows I had when I first knew the Lord was to think about certain individuals I had known. I knew right well that I had had ungodly conversations with some of them, and I had tempted various others to sin. One of the prayers that I always offered, when praying for myself, was that such a person would not be lost because of sins that I had tempted him to commit. This was the case also with George Whitefield, who never forgot those with whom he used to play cards before his conversion. He had the joy of leading every one of them to the Savior.

About five days after I first found Christ, when my joy had been so great that I could have danced for joy at the thought that Christ was mine, suddenly I fell into a sad fit of despondency. I now know why. When I first believed in Christ, I am not sure that I thought the Devil was dead, but certainly I had a kind of notion that he was so mortally wounded that he could not disturb me. And then I also imagined that the corruption of my nature had received its deathblow. I read what Cowper said:

> Since the dear hour that brought me to
> Thy foot
> And cut up all my follies by the root,

and I really thought that the poet knew what he was saying, whereas never did anyone blunder so terribly as Cowper did when he said that. No man, I think, has all his follies cut up by the roots.

However, I fondly dreamed that mine were; I was persuaded they would never sprout again. I was going to be perfect—I fully calculated on it—and, lo, I found an intruder I had not thought of: "an evil heart of unbelief, in departing from the living God" (Heb. 3:12).

So I went to that same Primitive Methodist chapel where I first received peace with God through the simple preaching of the Word. The text happened to be, "O wretched man that I am! who shall deliver me from the body of this death?" (Rom. 7:24).

"There," I thought, "that's the text for me." I had just gotten that far in a week. I knew that I had put my trust in Christ. I knew that, when I sat in that house of prayer, my faith was simply and solely fixed on the atonement of the Redeemer. But I had a weight on my mind because I could not be as holy as I

wanted to be. I could not live without sin.
When I rose in the morning, I thought I
would abstain from every harsh word,
from every evil thought and look; and I
came to that chapel groaning because
"when I would do good, evil [was] present
with me" (Rom. 7:21).

The minister began by saying, "Paul
was not a believer when he said this."
Well, now, I knew I was a believer, and it
seemed to me from the context that Paul
must have been a believer, too. (Now, I
am sure he was.) The man went on to say
that no child of God ever felt any conflict
within. So I took my hat and left the
chapel, and I have very seldom attended
such places since. They are very good for
people who are unconverted to go to but
of very little use for children of God.

That is my notion of Methodism. It is
a noble thing for strangers but a terrible
thing for those who need spiritual food. It
is like the parish pound: it is a good place
to put sheep in when they have strayed,
but there is no food inside. They had better be let out as soon as possible to find
some grass.

I saw that that minister understood nothing of experimental divinity or of practical heart theology; otherwise, he would not have talked as he did. I do not doubt he was a good man, but he was utterly incompetent for the task of dealing with a case like mine.

Oh, what a horror I have had of sin ever since the day when I felt its power over my soul! O sin, *sin,* I have had enough of you! You never did bring me more than a moment's seeming joy, and with it there came a deep and awful bitterness that burns within me to this day!

Well do I recollect when I was the subject of excessive tenderness—some people called it "morbid sensibility." How I shuddered and shivered at the very thought of sin, which then appeared exceedingly sinful! The first week after I was converted to God, I felt afraid to put one foot before the other for fear I should do wrong. When I thought over the day, if there had been a failure in my temper or if there had been a trifling word spoken or something done amiss, I did punish myself severely. At that time, if I had known anything to be my Lord's will, I think I would not have hesitated to do it. To me it would not have mattered whether it was a fashionable thing or an unfashionable thing, but only if it were according to His Word. Oh, to do His will! Oh, to follow Him wherever He wanted me to go! It seemed then as though I should never, never, never be slack in keeping His commandments.

I do not know whether the experiences of others agree with mine. However, the worst difficulty I ever met with, or I think I can ever meet with, happened a little time after my conversion to God. When I first knew the weight of sin, it was a burden, a labor, a trouble. Then I prayed that I might know the Lord better.

> I asked the Lord that I might grow,
> In faith, and love, and every
> grace,
> Might more of His salvation know,
> And seek more earnestly His
> face.

He answered me by letting all my sins loose upon me. Then they appeared more frightful than before. I thought the Egyptians in Egypt were not half as bad as the Egyptians out of Egypt. I thought the sins I knew before, though they were cruel taskmasters, were not half as much to be dreaded as those soldier-sins, armed with spears and axes, riding in iron chariots with scythes on their axles, hastening to assault me. It is true they did not come as near to me as before; nevertheless, they caused me even more fright than when I was their slave.

The Israelites went up wearing their armor, marching in their ranks, and, no doubt, singing as they went because they had been delivered from the daily task and from the cruel bondage. Suddenly, they turned their heads while they were marching, for they heard a dreadful noise behind them, a noise of chariots and of men shouting for battle. At last, when they could really see the Egyptians and the thick cloud of dust rising behind them, then they said that they would be destroyed, that they would now fall by the hand of the enemy. (See Exodus 14:10–12.)

I remember that after my conversion (it may not have happened to all, but it did to me) there came a time when the enemy said, "I will pursue, I will overtake, I will divide the spoil; my lust shall be satisfied upon them; I will draw my sword, my hand shall destroy them" (Exod. 15:9). So Satan, reluctant to leave a soul, pursues it speedily. He will have it back if he can; and often, soon after conversion, there comes a time of dreadful conflict when the soul seems as if it could not live.

"Was it because there were no graves in Egypt that the Lord brought us into this condition of temporary freedom, that we might be all the more distressed by our adversaries?" So said unbelief. God, however, brought His people right out by one final stroke. Miriam knew it when she took her tambourine, went forth with the women, and answered them in the jubilant song, "Sing ye to the LORD, for He hath triumphed gloriously; the horse and his rider hath he thrown into the sea" (Exod. 15:21).

I love best of all that note in the song of Moses where he says, "The depths have covered them" (Exod. 15:5). There remained not so much as one of them. What gladness must have been in the hearts of the children of Israel when they knew that their enemies were all gone! I am sure it was that way with me. For, after my conversion, being attacked by sin again, I saw the mighty stream of redeeming love roll over all my sins, and this was my song, "The depths have covered them."

> *Who shall lay any thing to the charge of God's elect? It is God that justifieth. Who is he that condemneth? It is Christ that died, yea rather, that is risen again, who is even at the right hand of God, who also maketh intercession for us.*
>
> *(Rom. 8:33–34)*

I was raised with such care that I heard very little foul or profane language, having hardly ever heard a man swear.

Yet, I remember times in my earliest Christian days when there came into my mind thoughts so evil that I clapped my hand over my mouth for fear I would utter them. This is one way in which Satan tortures those whom God has delivered out of his hand. Many of the choicest saints have been harassed this way.

Once, when I had been grievously attacked by the tempter, I went to see my dear old grandfather. I told him about my terrible experience, and then I wound up by saying, "Grandfather, I am sure I cannot be a child of God, or else I would never have such evil thoughts as these."

"Nonsense, Charles," answered the good old man. "It is because you are a Christian that you are tempted like this. These blasphemies are no children of yours; they are the Devil's brats, which he delights to lay at the door of a Christian. Don't you own them as yours; give them neither house room nor heart room."

I felt greatly comforted by what my grandfather said, especially since it confirmed what another old saint had told me when I was tempted in a similar manner while I was seeking the Savior.

Many people make fun of that verse,

'Tis a point I long to know,
    Oft it causes anxious thought,
Do I love the Lord, or no?
    Am I His, or am I not?

If they ever find themselves where some of us have been, they will not make fun of it anymore. I believe it is a shallow experience that makes people always confident of what they are and where they are, for there are times of terrible trouble that make even the most confident child of God hardly know whether he is on his head or on his heels. It is the sailor who has sailed on great waters who, in times of unusual stress and storm, reels to and fro, staggers like a drunken man, and is at his wits' end.

If Jesus whispers that I am His at such a time, then the question is answered once and for all. Then my soul has received a token that it waves in the

face of Satan, making him disappear.
Then I can go on my way rejoicing.

Chapter Five

Centering on Christ

I have found in my own spiritual life that the more rules I lay down for myself, the more sins I commit. The habit of regular morning and evening prayer is one that is indispensable to a believer's life; however, to prescribe the length of prayer and to try to remember many persons and subjects may lead to bondage and may strangle prayer rather than assist it.

To say I will humble myself at such a time and rejoice at such another season is almost as artificial as when the preacher wrote in the margin of his sermon, "Cry here," "Smile here." Why, if the man preached from his heart, he would be sure to cry in the right place and to smile at a suitable moment. Likewise, when the spiritual life is sound, it produces prayer at the right time; and humiliation of soul and sacred joy spring forth spontaneously, apart from rules and vows. The kind of religion that makes itself to order by the almanac and turns out its emotions like bricks from a machine, weeping on Good Friday and rejoicing two days afterwards, measuring its motions by the moon, is too artificial to be worthy of my imitation.

Self-examination is a very great blessing, but I have known self-examination to be carried on in a most unbelieving, legal, and self-righteous manner; in fact, I have done it that way myself. Time was when I used to think a vast deal more of marks and signs and evidences than I do now, for I find that I cannot be a match for the Devil when I begin dealing in these things. I am obliged to go from day to day with this cry:

I, the chief of sinners am,
But Jesus died for me.

All goes well with me when I believe the promise of God simply because it is His promise. All goes well when I trust my Savior simply because He is God and, therefore, mighty to save. I do find, however, when I begin questioning myself about this and that perplexity, thus taking my eye off Christ, that all the virtue of my life seems to ooze out at every pore. Any practice that detracts from faith is an evil practice, but that kind of self-examination that would take us away from the foot of the cross is especially misleading.

When I first knew the Savior, I used to examine myself in a certain manner. I often threw stumbling blocks in my path through it; therefore, I can warn any who are doing the same. Sometimes I would go up to my room, and by way of self-examination, I used to ask myself these questions: "Am I afraid to die? If I would drop down dead in my room, can I say that I would joyfully close my eyes?"

Well, it often happened that I could not honestly say so. I used to feel that death would be a very solemn thing. "Ah, then!" I said, "I have never believed in Christ; for if I had put my trust in the Lord Jesus, I would not be afraid to die, but I would be quite confident."

I do not doubt that many people are saying, "I cannot follow Christ because I am afraid to die. I cannot believe that Jesus Christ will save me because the thought of death makes me tremble." Ah, poor soul, there are many of God's blessed ones who through fear of death have spent much of their lifetime in bondage! I know precious children of God that I believe will die triumphantly when they die, but I know that the thought of death is never pleasing to them.

This fear of death can be accounted for by the fact that God has stamped on nature a law; it is the law of love of life and self-preservation. It is natural enough that the man who has kindred and friends would hardly like to leave behind those who are so dear. I know that when he gets more grace, he will rejoice in the thought of death; but I do know that there are many quite safe who will die rejoicing in Christ, but who now, in the prospect of death, feel afraid of it.

My aged grandfather once preached a sermon that I have never forgotten. He was preaching from the text, "The God of all grace" (1 Pet. 5:10). After describing the different kinds of grace that God gave, he somewhat interested the assembly by saying at the end of each period, "But there is one kind of grace that you do not want." After each part of his theme, there came the same sentence, "But there is one kind of grace that you do not want." And then he wound up by saying, "You don't want dying grace in living moments, but you will have dying grace when you need it. When you are in the condition that requires it, you will have grace enough if you put your trust in Christ."

In a group of friends, we were discussing the question of whether we were prepared to be burned if the days of martyrdom came. I said, "I must frankly tell you that, speaking as I feel today, I am not prepared to be burned. But I do believe that if there were a stake at Smithfield, and I knew that I were to be burned there at one o'clock, I would have enough grace to be burned there when one o'clock came."

In my younger days, I was much impressed by hearing a minister, blind with age, speak at the communion table. He told us who had just joined the church that it was good that we had come to put our trust in a faithful God. As the good man, with great feebleness and yet with great earnestness, said to us that he had never regretted giving himself to Christ as a boy, I felt my heart leap within me with delight that I had such a God to be my God.

A younger man could not have given that testimony. He might have spoken more fluently, but the weight of those eighty years at the back of it made the old man eloquent to my young heart. For twenty years, he had not seen the light of the sun. His snow-white hair hung from his brow and floated over his shoulders. He stood up at the table of the Lord and addressed us with these words: "Brothers and sisters, I will soon be taken from you. In a few more months, I will lie down on my bed and sleep with my fathers. I do not have the mind of the learned nor the tongue of the eloquent; but I desire, before I go, to bear one public testimony to my God. Fifty-six years I have served Him, and I have never once found Him unfaithful. I can say, 'Surely goodness and mercy [have followed] me all the days of my life' (Ps. 23:6), and 'not one thing hath failed of all the good things which the LORD [my] God [promised]' (Josh. 23:14)."

There stood that dear old man, tottering into his tomb, naturally deprived of the light of heaven, and yet having the Light of Heaven in a better sense shining into his soul. Though he could not look upon us, he turned towards us, and he seemed to say, "Young people, trust God in early life, for I do not have the regret that I sought Him too soon. I only mourn that so many of my years went to waste."

There is nothing that tends to strengthen the faith of the young believer more than to hear the veteran Christian, covered with scars from the battle, say, "The service of my Master is a happy service. If I could have served any other master, I would not have done so; for His service is pleasant, and His reward is everlasting joy."

In my early days, I knew a good man who has now gone to his reward, who was the means of producing, under God, a library of useful lives. I do not mean books in paper, but books in boots! Many young men came to the Lord by his means, and they became preachers, teachers, deacons, and other workers. No one would be amazed at this if he knew the man who trained them. He was ready for every good word and work, but he gave special attention to his Bible class, in which he presented the Gospel with clearness and zeal.

Whenever any one of his young men left the country town in which he lived, he would be sure to arrange a parting interview. There was a wide-spreading oak down in the fields, and there he was accustomed to keeping an early morning appointment with John or Thomas or William. That appointment consisted of a great deal of earnest pleading with the Lord that, in going up to the great city, the young man might be kept from sin and be made useful. Under that tree, several decided to come to the Savior. It was an impressive act and left its influence on them, for many men came in later years to see the spot made sacred by their teacher's prayers.

Oh, how my young heart ached this one time in boyhood soon after I came to love the Savior. I was far away from father and mother and all I loved, and I thought my heart would break. I was an usher in a school, in a place where I could find little sympathy or help. Well, I went to my room and told my little griefs into the ears of Jesus. They were great griefs to me then, though they are nothing now. When on my knees, I just whispered them into the ear of Him who had loved me with an everlasting love. Oh, it was so sweet! If I had told them to others, they would have repeated them; but He, my blessed Confidant, knows all my secrets, and He never repeats them.

There is one verse of Scripture that, as a young believer, I used to repeat often, for it was very dear to me. It is this: "Bind the sacrifice with cords, even unto the horns of the altar" (Ps. 118:27). I did feel then that I was wholly Christ's. In the marriage covenant of which the Lord speaks, when the Husband put the ring upon His bride's finger, He said to her, "You have become Mine." I remember when I felt upon my finger the ring of infinite, everlasting, covenant love that Christ put there. Oh, it was a joyful day, a blessed day! Happy day, happy day, when His choice was known to me, and He fixed my choice on Him! That blessed rest of soul that comes from a sure possession of Christ is not to be imitated, but it is greatly to be desired.

I know that some good people, who I believe will be saved, nevertheless do not attain to this sweet rest. They keep on thinking that it is something that they may get when they are very old or when they are about to die; but they look upon the full assurance of faith and the personal grasping of Christ and saying, "My beloved is mine" (Song 2:16), as something very dangerous.

I began my Christian life in a happy fashion as a boy, fifteen years of age. I believed fully and without hesitation in the Lord Jesus Christ. When I went to see a good Christian woman, I was simple enough to tell her that I believed in Christ, that He was mine, and that He had saved me. I expressed myself very confidently concerning the great truth that God would never forsake His people nor leave His work undone.

The good woman at once scolded me and told me that I had no right to speak so confidently, for it was presumptuous. She said to me, "Ah! I don't like such assurance as that." Then she added, "I trust you are believing in Christ—I hope so—but I have never got beyond a hope or a trust, and I am an old woman."

Bless the old woman, she was no example for us who "know whom [we] have believed" (2 Tim. 1:12). We ought to rise far above that groveling kind of life. The man who begins right, the boy who begins right, and the girl who begins right will begin by saying, "God has said it: 'He that believeth on him is not condemned' (John 3:18). I believe on Him; therefore, I am not condemned. Christ is mine."

Before my conversion, I was accustomed to reading the Scriptures to admire their grandeur, to feel the charm of their history, and to wonder at the majesty of their language; but I altogether missed the Lord's intent therein. But when the Spirit came with His divine life and quickened all of the Book to my newly enlightened soul, the inner meaning shone forth with wondrous glory.

I was not in a frame of mind to judge God's Word; I accepted it all without hesitation. I did not venture to sit in judgment upon my Judge. I did not dare to become the reviser of the unerring God. Whatever I found to be in His Word, I received with intense joy.

I thank God that I have been happy from that hour. I am not saying that I am exempt from trouble. I am especially not free from a tendency to despondency that is always with me. However, I rejoice and will rejoice. I am happy, unspeakably happy, in resting upon Jesus Christ. Moreover, I have found that those points of my character that were most weak have been strengthened, while strong passions have been subdued, evil tendencies have been kept under, and new principles have been implanted.

I am changed. I am as different from what I was as a man who had been annihilated and had then been made over again. I do not claim any of the credit for this change—far from it. God has done great things for me, but He has done the same for others. He is willing to do great things for any soul that seeks His face through Jesus Christ and His great atoning sacrifice.

I have known some men who were almost mentally retarded before conversion, but afterwards they had their faculties wonderfully developed. Some time ago, there was a man who was so uneducated that he could not read. He never spoke anything close to proper grammar in his life, unless by mistake. But when he was converted, the first thing he did was pray. He stammered out a few words, and in a little time his powers of speaking began to develop themselves. Then he thought he would like to read the Scriptures. After long, long months of labor, he learned to read. And what was the next thing? He thought he could preach. He did preach a little, in his own simple way, in his house. Then he thought, "I must read a few more books." And so his mind expanded. I believe that now he is a useful minister, settled in a country village, laboring for God.

An idea has long possessed the public mind that a religious man can hardly be a wise man. It has been the custom to talk of infidels, atheists, and deists as men of deep thought and comprehensive intellect and, at the same time, to tremble for the Christian controversialist as if he must surely fall by the hand of his enemy. But this is purely a mistake. The Gospel is the sum of wisdom, an epitome of knowledge, a treasure-house of truth, and a revelation of mysterious secrets. In it, we see how justice and mercy may be married. Here we behold unbending law entirely satisfied and sovereign love bearing away the sinner in triumph. Our meditation upon it enlarges the mind. As the Gospel opens to our soul in successive flashes of glory, we stand astonished at the profound wisdom manifested in it.

I have often said that before I knew the Gospel, I had gathered up a jumbled mass of all kinds of knowledge from here, there, and everywhere—a bit of chemistry, a bit of botany, a bit of astronomy, and a bit of this, that, and the other. I put them all together in one great confused chaos. But when I learned the Gospel, I got a shelf in my head on which to put everything just where it should be.

It seemed to me as if, when I had discovered Christ and Him crucified, I had found the center of the system so that I could see every other science revolving in due order. From the earth, the planets appear to move in a very irregular manner; they are progressive, retrograde, or stationary. But if you could stand on the sun, you would see them marching around in their constant, uniform, circular motion.

So it is with knowledge. Begin with any other science you like, and truth will seem to be all awry. Begin with the science of Christ crucified, and you will begin with the sun; you will see every other science moving around it in complete harmony.

The greatest mind in the world will be developed by beginning at the right end. The old saying is, "Go from nature up to nature's God," but it is hard work going uphill. The best thing is to go from nature's God down to nature. If you once get to nature's God and believe Him and love Him, it is surprising how easy it is to hear music in the waves and songs in the wild whisperings of the winds. If you believe in God, it is easy to see God everywhere—in the stones, in the rocks, in the rippling brooks. It is easy to hear Him everywhere—in the lowing of cattle, in the rolling of thunders, and in the fury of tempests.

Christ is to me the wisdom of God. I can learn everything now that I know the science of Christ crucified.